FOUNDER LED
SALES

The Sales Handbook
for Startup Founders

Neeraj Sabharwal

Table Of Contents

1   Welcome Message

2   Introduction

3   What is a Sales Funnel?

4   MQL + SQL

5   TOFU Focus

6   Method Overview

7   Ideal Customer Profile

8   Identifying Targets

9   Product Messaging

10   The Golden Circle

11   Pitch Delivery

12   Outreach

13   Hunters and Hustlers

14   The Eagle Eye

15   A Founder's Story

16   Inbound Strategy

17   Benefits of Advertising

18   The Point of Social Media

19   Social Media Strategy

20   Leads on LinkedIn

21   Authenticity

22   What Comes Next?

Are you a founder feeling the customer acquisition struggle?

Let's cut to the chase!

Imagine your sales journey like a blockbuster movie. The Top of the Funnel (TOFU) is your opening scene - the hook that pulls folks in. First, you have to be where the action is. Social media, SEO, content marketing - spread your net wide.

Content is your main character. Make it the billboard that turns heads - short, snappy, and impossible to scroll past. No one wants a novel at a BBQ, right? Same deal online.

But here's the kicker - it's not a one-shot deal. TOFU is your grand entrance, not the grand finale. Follow-ups, emails/calls - be that friendly neighbor with the cookies. Keep the buzz alive.

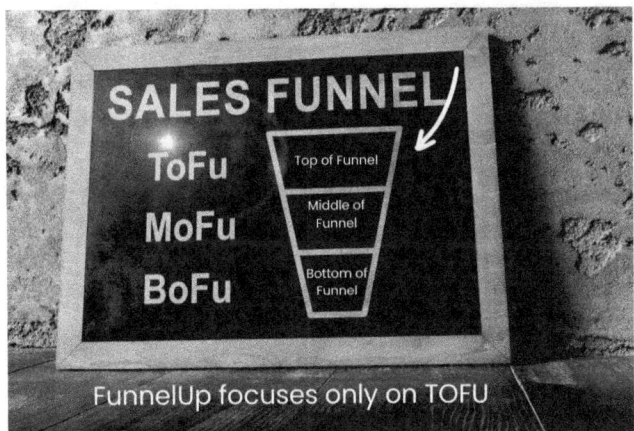

REVAMP YOUR SALES GAME IN JUST 30 MINUTES OF READING!

Turning an idea into a reality is like wrestling a wild bull – tough, but oh-so-rewarding. I've been in the trenches, faced my fair share of face-plants, but dang, did persistence pay off!

Picture this: $10 million in sales, $3 million in commissions – not too shabby for a tech enthusiast, right? Well, let me take you on a rollercoaster through my 24-year tech odyssey.

Started as a tech whiz 24 years ago, elbows deep in engineering. Data was my jam – databases, data centers, big data, you name it. But here's the twist – as the industry did the cha-cha, so did I. From security to the flashy world of low-code, I rode the tech wave like a champ.

But here's the secret sauce: I didn't stop at just geeking out on tech. Nope, I morphed into a business whisperer. Understanding the dance between tech and business transformation became my groove. Different avenues, different dances – but always moving forward. Trials, errors, face-plants – they were my boot camp. I didn't just survive; I thrived. Now, I'm here, grinning at $10 million in sales, $3 million in commissions, and a trail of tech adventures behind me.

So, if you're in the thick of it, sweating it out, just remember – persistence is the name of the game. Here's to turning dreams into dollar signs and tech journeys into success stories! Stepping into the world of sales engineering was like building a bridge – a connection between tech wizardry and business brilliance. My technical know-how became my secret weapon, understanding clients' needs, and dishing out solutions like a tech-savvy superhero.

I wasn't just talking in code; I learned the language of business. Translating tech jargon into the sweet melody of business value became my forte. It was like turning binary into a symphony that my clients could dance to. But hey, life's a journey, right? So, I decided to take the plunge into full-time sales. Building relationships, chasing goals – it was a shift, no doubt. Yet, my engineering roots gave me a superpower: a unique perspective and a killer set of skills that made the transition a breeze. Fast forward to today, and I'm feeling downright grateful for the twists and turns. My problem-solving skills, born in the engineering trenches, are now the compass guiding clients to their business nirvana. Building relationships isn't just a job; it's my love language. Seeing the impact of my work on clients' success? Now, that's the real deal.

Life's a journey, my friend, and I'm just getting started – armed with tech prowess, business savvy, and a whole lot of heart.

BASICS

What is a Sales Funnel?

A sales funnel is the path a potential customer takes from not knowing you to becoming a paying customer. It's like a journey from clueless to "shut up and take my money." Simple as that!

TWO CRUCIAL KEYWORDS FOR YOUR NEXT STEPS

Marketing Qualified Lead (MQL)

Sales Qualified Lead (SQL)

Listen up, folks! MQL, aka Marketing Qualified Lead, is your potential customer who's raised their hand and said, "Hey, I'm interested!" They've filled forms, downloaded white papers – basically, they're peeking through the window, curious about what you've got.

Now, here's the gold mine – SQL, or Sales Qualified Lead. These are the hotshots, the ones who've not just peeked but knocked on the door. They're showing serious interest, and we're talking engagement, budget, company size – the whole shebang. Passing these gems to sales for some TLC means focusing on high-quality leads and hitting that sweet spot with your ideal customer. It's like separating the wheat from the chaff and serving up the cream of the crop to your sales team. Quality over quantity, baby!

FunnelUp focuses solely on TOFU/MQLs.

4

FunnelUp

Founders, here's your reminder:

Alright, captain of the startup ship!

In the early days, you wear all the hats – from the CEO crown to the janitor's cap. The name of the game?

Top of the Funnel (TOFU) focus. It's like planting seeds – takes time and cash, but it's the foundation.

Now, if you've got heavy hitters like a VP of Marketing and Product Marketing (hello, big guns!), they're burning dollars in this zone. No room for trial and error.
We gotta nail it on the first swing.

So, here's the plan – let's team up and use this guide like our startup GPS. It's the secret sauce to get that top-of-the-funnel magic right from the get-go. Time to roll up those sleeves and make this startup journey a success!

CUTTING TO THE CHASE: ACTION TIME!

So, buckle up for my fab four pillars! I'm not just talking; I'm walking the walk. With my experience, approach, and ideas, I'm your go-to value delivery person. Let's turn those ideas into real-deal wins!

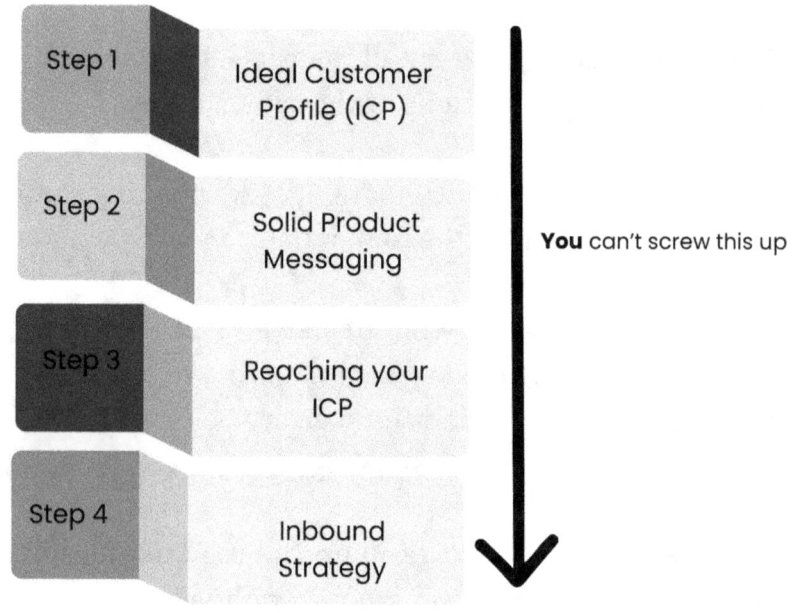

Step 1 — Ideal Customer Profile (ICP)

Step 2 — Solid Product Messaging

Step 3 — Reaching your ICP

Step 4 — Inbound Strategy

You can't screw this up

Time for a deep dive! Let's unravel these core concepts so you're crystal clear.

ICP

IDEAL CUSTOMER PROFILE

Ready to hit the sales jackpot? It's ICP magic time!

You nailed it! ICP is your sales team's golden ticket – a detailed roadmap to the dream customers.

Picture this: You're selling a security product; your ICP isn't just anyone. It's the VIPs – CISO, VP/Director of Security. No more shooting in the dark; it's all about hitting the bullseye with precision.

Important:

Launching a business isn't a walk in the park, especially rounding up those first customers.

Pro tip? Start local before going global. Why?

Testing the waters close by is like a warm-up – fewer headaches, fewer costs. Let's own the neighborhood before taking over the world.

STEP 1 - IDENTIFY TARGET BUSINESSES

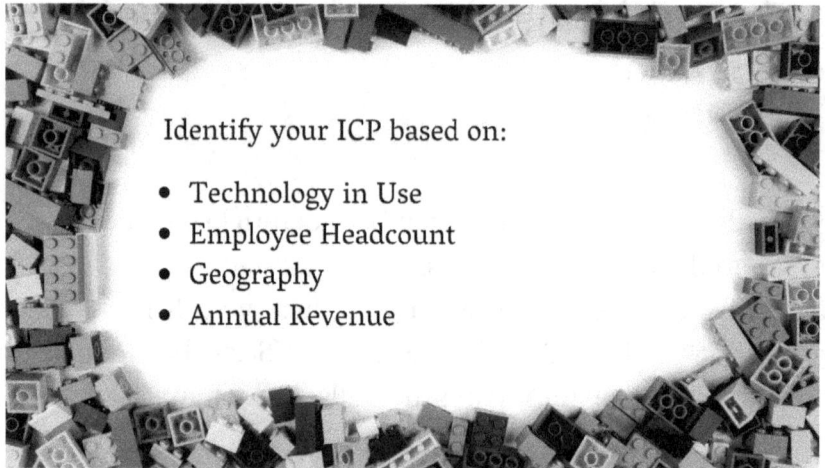

Identify your ICP based on:

- Technology in Use
- Employee Headcount
- Geography
- Annual Revenue

Crack the code on your target business!

Here's the scoop: the type of business you aim for depends on your product's stage. We're talking Enterprises (big dogs), Mid-Market (the middleweights), and SMB (the small fries).

Now, if you're in the hustle for those first customers and want a speedy sales cycle, think Mid-Market or SMB. It's like choosing the right tool for the job – a bit smaller, a lot faster. Let's snag those early wins without diving into the deep end.

STEP 2 - MESSAGING

Listen up, folks!

Your product messaging is the unsung hero in the sales saga. It's how you paint your product as the superhero in a market full of sidekicks.

Craft it like a masterpiece – clear, concise, and shouting your product's unique perks from the rooftops.

But here's the kicker: tailor that messaging to fit the buyer's journey. It's like having different outfits for different occasions. From waving the "Hey, look at me!" flag to sealing the deal – your messaging should be the MVP at every stage based on the person on the other side.

Now, starting the conversation? It's like a first date – make it count! Three minutes or less to impress, so be prepped, know your script, and hit the ground running.

Oh, and here's a golden rule: selling is a two-way street. You've got ears – use them! Listen to your prospect, tweak your message accordingly, and voila – you're not just selling; you're building trust and paving the way for a successful love story with your product.

Messaging 101: Start with Your "Why"

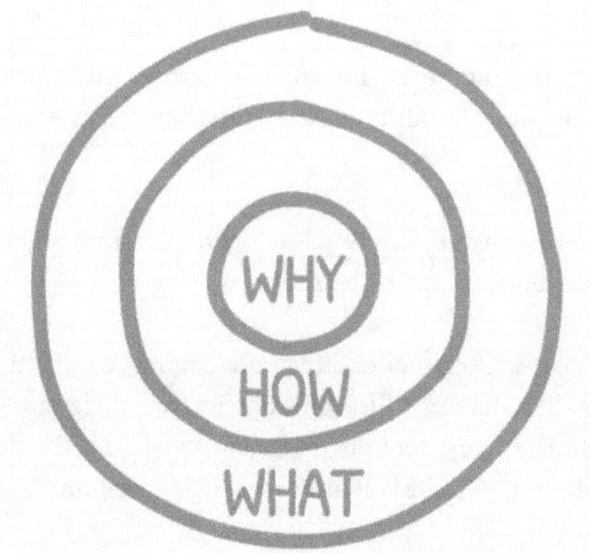

Source: https://simonsinek.com/golden-circle/

Absolutely spot on! Always kick off with your "Why."

It's like the North Star guiding your ship.

Simon Sinek's Golden Circle is your secret weapon – helping you communicate purpose, stand out, and light that fire under your audience.

I get it; the shift from engineering to sales had me diving into tech talk too. But here's the wisdom – taking a minute to lay down the "Why" changes the game. It's like setting the stage before the main act. I even drop the Golden Circle nugget in my chats with customers, subtly weaving purpose into the conversation.

So, remember, whether in your head or in the room, starting with the "Why" is the magic spell for that deep connection. Let your purpose shine and watch the sparks fly!

Instead of this...	Say this:
How and What	Start with Why
My product delivers better data security because we use better technology. As you know the data security is important component of any enterprise. Let me show you how it works.	Why: Data security has become a major concern for individuals and businesses. With the increasing amount of data being generated and stored, the risk of data breaches and cyber attacks is at an all-time high. How: That's why it's important to invest in a product that offers top-notch data security. What: My product is designed to deliver the highest level of data security. Our team of experts has developed advanced encryption algorithms that ensure your data is protected from unauthorized access. Whether you're storing sensitive personal information or confidential business data, our product provides a secure solution for all your data storage needs. Don't take chances with your data security. Invest in our product today and experience the best data security solution available in the market.
My product solves better data integration with other data sources. We have 50+ connectors.	Why: With the rise of big data, organizations are constantly looking for ways to integrate and make sense of the vast amounts of information available to them. How: This is where organization want faster and cheaper way integrate large data sets What: That's where our product comes in. Our solution provides seamless data integration with over 50 connectors to various data sources. This means that organizations can easily pull in data from multiple sources, allowing for more comprehensive analysis and insights. With our solution, organizations can make better-informed decisions and stay ahead of the competition in today's data-driven world.

STEP 3: REACHING

No good messaging, no scalable sales model. It's the backbone, not the cherry on top.

Founders, buckle up – your Everest is time and money. Your mission? Get eyes on your site, blog, or any content hub. Then, the real ninja move – turn those eyeballs into calls with you or your sales squad. It's the ultimate challenge, but conquer it, and you're on the road to victory. Time to hustle!

Founders, listen up! Want folks flooding your site and ringing your sales bell? Here's the playbook:

Step 1: Pump out **valuable content** like there's no tomorrow. Blogs, social media, videos – be the content maestro. Show your audience you're the real deal, and trust will follow.

Step 2: Network like a champ! Hit up industry events, dive into social media groups, and make it personal. **Build a community** around your brand, and watch the magic happen.

Step 3: Once you've got eyeballs, **seal the deal**. Offer freebies, host webinars, or just straight-up ask for that call. It's the final dance move in the sales tango.

Remember, relationships and value are your secret weapons. Serve 'em up, and watch your brand become the talk of the town. Time to make those connections and turn heads!

As a founder of an early stage startup or sales leader, you need hunters and hustlers.

Hunters

Meet the **hunters in sales** – the real go-getters of the game. These folks are like the bloodhounds of opportunity, always sniffing out new clients and chasing down fresh deals. They thrive on the chase, are risk-takers, and put in the elbow grease to seal the deal.

Communication and interpersonal skills? Check! Hunters are maestros at building killer client relationships. But hold up – there's a counterpart in this sales safari: the farmers. They're all about tending to existing relationships.

Now, don't get it twisted – both roles are crucial. But let's be real, hunters are the growth catalysts, the driving force behind expanding that customer base. It's all about the thrill of the chase and bagging those wins!

Hustlers

Say hello to the **hustlers** in sales – the unstoppable force ready to do whatever it takes! These folks are the persistent, creative, and resourceful warriors not fazed by rejection. Working overtime, making those extra calls – they're in it to win it.

But it's not just about the grind. Hustlers are relationship wizards. Networking is their jam, and they can charm even the toughest clients. Charismatic, confident, and persuasive – they're the closer squad.

Now, here's the secret sauce: combine the hunters (the opportunity scouts) with the hustlers (the deal-closers), and you've got a dream team. One finds the leads, the other seals the deals. Together, they're the dynamic duo that can shoot your startup to the stars.

You cannot succeed to take your company to the next level without these qualities in your founding sales team.

Founders must have the "Eagle Eye" to find hustlers.

You need someone who is not only **passionate** about your product but also has the **skills** to take it to the next level.

A hustler is someone who can **work tirelessly** to make your product successful. They have the ability to identify and seize opportunities that others may overlook. It's important to find someone who shares your vision and is willing to put in the hard work to make it a reality.

 Look for someone who is creative, resourceful, and able to adapt quickly to changes in the market. With the right hustler by your side, you can take your product to new heights and achieve the success you've always dreamed of.

PERSONAL STORY

Being a part of an early-stage startup was an incredible experience. As the second employee, I was able to see the company grow and transform from its very beginnings. It was a time of great uncertainty, as we were operating without any venture capital funding and had to rely solely on our own resources and ingenuity to keep the business afloat.

Despite the challenges, we persevered and slowly but surely made progress. We worked tirelessly to build our product, refine our strategy, and acquire customers. It was a rollercoaster ride, with many ups and downs along the way, but it was also incredibly rewarding to see our hard work pay off.

Over time, we were able to secure funding and expand our team, which allowed us to accelerate our growth even further. And before we knew it, we had gone from a preseed startup with just $50k in revenue to a series B company with $12 million in annual recurring revenue.

Looking back on the journey, I feel a sense of pride and accomplishment. It was a privilege to be a part of such a dynamic and innovative team, and to witness the incredible progress we made together. I learned so much from the experience, and it has shaped who I am as both a professional and a person.

Remember, the foundation of everything is Messaging/Why. Then you evolve from there.

Imagine this kid in the pool is you, the founder. The kid swimming next to you in the other swim-lane is your hustler. Together, you are swimming parallel and building your inbound strategy.

Step 4: Inbound Strategy

Ready for the million-dollar question? How to generate inbound without breaking the bank? Easy hack: Boost that brand awareness!

In today's dog-eat-dog market, brand awareness is your secret sauce. It's about how much customers recognize and remember your brand. The more visible you are, the more customers you attract and keep.

Ways to crank up brand awareness? Nail that brand identity, rock social media, join events, and sprinkle in some smart advertising. Build a solid brand presence, boost credibility, and voila – trust builds, sales spike.

So, if you're a business owner eyeing an easier life, time to go all-in on cranking up that brand awareness.

Benefits of Advertising 101:
Get ready to boost your brand game!

Advertising isn't just a move; it's the game-changer for brand awareness. Do it right, and you'll see the magic unfold. It's a cost-effective powerhouse if you play your cards smart. But, and here's the kicker, don't rely on others blindly unless you've got a true hustler in your marketing squad.

Every action that you are going to take after reading this will improve your brand awareness.

Now, let me drop some knowledge. I once tossed $300 into a Google ad, got a bunch of irrelevant inquiries, but guess what? I closed deals worth $90,000 USD.

No coincidence – pure strategy. **Advertising is your secret weapon**, and here's why it works like a charm. $300 Google ad. Got inquiries, closed a $90,000 deal. Short, sweet, sales magic!

Picture this – had this epic sales call recently, a real game-changer! So, this prospect hits my calendar link, we're in business. Pitching our top-notch tech-based product, right? Started off with the Golden Circle vibe, breaking down the why behind our tech wizardry. Showed him the productivity jackpot we're packing, dropped a hint to rethink his old-school strategy. His questions screamed "tradition," so I nudged him towards the light.

Kicked it off by talking business value. No tech lingo, just savings, productivity gains – the whole value-packed shabang. Made it a breeze for him to chat with management. We're not just selling tech; we're selling a game-changing conversation starter. Mic drop!

17

Let's talk about social media investments – every dollar should be a brand boost!

Social media, especially LinkedIn, might sting the wallet, but trust me, it's a powerhouse for brand elevation. Facebook and LinkedIn, with their gazillion users, are your golden gates to potential customers.

Now, here's the secret sauce: social media ads aren't just about selling; they're about engaging. It's a relationship game. Follow these tips, and you'll craft ads that don't just talk but resonate, expanding your business like wildfire. Social media mastery, unlocked!

Social Media Strategy

Alright, buckle up for some tested-and-proven wisdom that gets the job done:

LinkedIn Wisdom: Organic Leads Magic:

Don't shy away from putting yourself in the spotlight! As a founder, CEO, or co-founder, your title is a goldmine. Share your thoughts, spill those ideas – people are hungry for it. Trust me, your voice matters more than you think.

Social Media Gold Mine: Pages Unleashed:

Your LinkedIn company page, Facebook business page, and Instagram account are your secret weapons. They're not just pages; they're marketing powerhouses. Minimal investment, maximum results. But, beware of the neglectful marketing leaders – keep an eagle eye on that traffic or risk burning cash.
Time to shine bright on LinkedIn and make those social media pages work like a charm!

It's time to hustle.

Alright, time to unleash the Hustler and let the magic unfold! The hunter hat is on, and it's digging season.

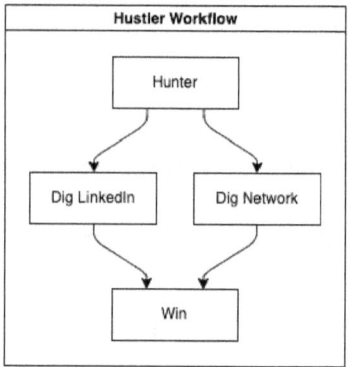

As the founder or sales leader, here's the playbook: Hustler, dive deep into LinkedIn. Tap into 1st, 2nd, and 3rd degree connections. It's not just networking; it's a gold mine waiting to be uncovered. Let the connections lead the way to sales glory!

LinkedIn – the sales ninja's ultimate weapon! Time to unlock its power.

Tell your hunter to dive deep into the 1st, 2nd, and 3rd degree connections on LinkedIn. It's like having a secret passage to an endless pool of prospects, ones your team might've missed.

But here's the kicker: personalization is the key. Urge your hunter to craft outreach messages that scream sincerity. Building relationships is the game-changer. Trust and credibility – that's the currency.

And wait, there's more! LinkedIn is a treasure trove of insights. Job titles, company size, interests – it's a goldmine. Your team can tailor their approach, armed with data that hits the bullseye.

LinkedIn, the unsung hero in your sales arsenal. Unleash the hunter, and let the connections lead the way to sales victory!

In a nutshell, LinkedIn connections are your sales strategy's MVP. Unleash your hunter, tap into that magic network, and let the sales show begin!

And hey, seriously, don't just skim – read read this article
like it's the key to the treasure chest!

Time for a heart-to-heart on authenticity!

Why Genuine Connections Matter: A Founder's Tale

Let me spill the beans on my "genuine" obsession. Recently, a founder hit me up, praising the vibe in my approach compared to other sales folks. While I'm all about authentic connections, others seem laser-focused on sealing the deal.

As a founder or leader, you have to set the tone. Take a beat, listen, and truly understand your prospects. Spark that curiosity, show genuine interest – it's the secret sauce. Before you start your spiel, remember: listening is the golden ticket to relationships that stand the test of time.

Here is a key:

"With people fast is slow and slow is fast." - Stephen R. Covey

I follow this always in life. Let me give you my way of translating this.

When you meet new people (prospects), you should take time to know them. If you are on a call for 25 minutes, set the context this way:

"I know we have only 25 mins and my main goal in this call is to know more about you and your needs to see how I can be helpful to you. Are you ok if I ask you a few questions after the introductions?"

Tips for Successful Sales: Remain composed and unhurried, so that your potential customer sees you as a confident salesperson, rather than someone who is desperate.

You've set up the ads, and the hustler is on the hunt. What comes next?

Having that burning desire?

It's like having a secret weapon – the key to unlocking dreams. When life throws curveballs, that fire is what keeps you swinging. Think about it – are you ready to roll up your sleeves, dive into the hustle, and make those dreams happen? If the answer's a big fat yes, then let that burning desire be your turbo boost to success. It's not just about dreaming; it's about getting down and dirty, conquering your destiny.

Now, in the world of sales, it's all about growing that network. No more waiting around – actively hunt those opportunities. Outbound calls might feel like a wild ride, but that's where the magic happens. Push your team, maybe throw in a BDR for some extra firepower – because expanding your network is all about grinding it out.

So, when it comes to chasing dreams and making those sales moves, let that burning desire be your guiding star. Dreams don't sprout from sitting around; they ignite in the heat of your fiery ambitions. It's not just about dreaming – it's about being a doer, seizing your destiny. Time to step up, be the ultimate dream chaser and conqueror!

"A BURNING DESIRE TO BE, AND TO DO is the starting point from which the dreamer must take off. Dreams are not born of indifference, laziness, or lack of ambition." — **Napoleon Hill, Think and Grow Rich**

Connect with me

Neeraj Sabharwal

Email: n333sab@gmail.com